A 6-Month Guide to
BETTER
PRAYER

A 6-Month
Guide to
BETTER
PRAYER

VALUEBOOKS
An Imprint of Barbour Publishing, Inc.

© 2009 by Barbour Publishing, Inc.

Print ISBN 978-1-63058-665-2

eBook editions:
Adobe Digital Edition (.epub) 978-1-63409-164-0
Kindle and MobiPocket Edition (.prc) 978-1-63409-165-7

Published by Value Books, an imprint of Barbour Publishing, Inc., P.O. Box 719, Uhrichsville, Ohio 44683, www.barbourbooks.com

Our mission is to publish and distribute inspirational products offering exceptional value and biblical encouragement to the masses.

ecpa Member of the
Evangelical Christian
Publishers Association

Printed in the United States of America.

CONTENTS

INTRODUCTION

*The story of prayer
is the story of great achievements.*
E. M. BOUNDS

As water is to physical life, so prayer is to spiritual life. Prayer is the basic element that energizes and refreshes our spiritual life. It's not too much to say that prayer allows our spiritual life to exist—without it, we wither and crumble inside.

Though at its most basic level prayer is simply talking to God, the Bible contains many instructions and examples for improving this vital process. Over the centuries, godly men and women have studied and applied those biblical passages, explaining them in writing for the benefit of others. This little book contains some of their insights.

This *6-Month Guide to Better Prayer* features a chapter for each month, drawn from the powerful writings of the following individuals:

- E. M. Bounds (1835–1913)—American minister and author of several books on prayer

- François Fénelon (1651–1715) and Madame Jeanne Guyon (1648–1717)—French theologians and writers
- Andrew Murray (1828–1917)—South African theologian and prayer expert
- Charles H. Spurgeon (1834–1892)—British preacher and writer
- R. A. Torrey (1856–1928)—American evangelist and writer
- George Whitefield (1714–1770)—British evangelist

Each entry has been lightly updated for ease of reading.

Classic Christian writings can certainly enhance your spiritual life, but should always be read in conjunction with the Bible. We suggest that you use one chapter of this book per month, reading it each day. Then, in your own copy of scripture, begin to review the verses and references in the text.

Make each chapter the basis of a monthly Bible study, and put into practice the truths you find. By year's end, your prayer life will undoubtedly be fresher, stronger, and more real than ever before.

1.
PRAYER—ITS POSSIBILITIES
E. M. BOUNDS

Open your mouth wide,
and I will fill it.
PSALM 81:10

How vast are the possibilities of prayer! How wide is its reach! What great things are accomplished by this divinely appointed means of grace! It lays its hand on Almighty God and moves Him to do what He would not otherwise do if prayer was not offered. It brings things to pass which would never otherwise occur. The story of prayer is the story of great achievements. Prayer is a wonderful power placed by Almighty God in the hands of His saints, which may be used to accomplish great purposes and to achieve unusual results. Prayer reaches to everything, takes in all things great and small which are promised by God to the children of men. The only limits to prayer are the promises of

God and His ability to fulfill those promises. "Open your mouth wide, and I will fill it" (Psalm 81:10).

The records of prayer's achievements are encouraging to faith, cheering to the expectations of saints, and an inspiration to all who would pray and test its value.

Prayer is no mere untried theory. It is not some strange unique scheme, concocted in the brains of men and set on foot by them, an invention which has never been tried nor put to the test. Prayer is a divine arrangement in the moral government of God, designed for the benefit of men and intended as a means for furthering the interests of His cause on earth and carrying out His gracious purposes in redemption and providence. Prayer proves itself. It is susceptible of proving its virtue by those who pray. Prayer needs no proof other than its accomplishments.

"If anyone wills to do His will, he shall know concerning the doctrine" (John 7:17). If any man will know the virtue of prayer, if he will know what it will do, let him pray. Let him put prayer to the test.

What a breadth is given to prayer! What heights it reaches! It is the breathing of a soul inflamed for God and inflamed for man. It goes as far as the gospel goes, and is as wide, compassionate, and prayerful as is that gospel.

How much of prayer do all these unpossessed, alienated provinces of earth demand in order to enlighten them, to impress them, and to move them toward God and His Son, Jesus Christ? Had the professed disciples of Christ only have prayed in the past as they ought to have done, the centuries would not have found these provinces still bound in death, in sin, and in ignorance.

Alas! how the unbelief of men has limited the power of God to work through prayer! What limitations have disciples of Jesus Christ put upon prayer by their prayerlessness! How the Church, with her neglect of prayer, has hedged about the gospel and shut up doors of access!

Prayer possibilities open doors for the entrance of the gospel: "meanwhile praying also for us, that God would open to us a door forthe word" (Colossians 4:3). Prayer opened for the apostles doors for the Word, created opportunities, and made openings to preach the gospel. The appeal by prayer was to God, because God was moved by prayer. God was thereby moved to do His own work in an enlarged way and by new ways. Prayer possibility gives not only great power, and opens doors to the gospel, but gives facility as well to the gospel. Prayer makes the gospel to go fast and to move with glorious fastness. A gospel projected by the mighty energies of prayer is neither slow, lazy, nor dull. It moves with God's power, with God's effulgence, and with angelic swiftness.

"Brethren, pray for us, that the word of the Lord may run swiftly and be glorified" (2 Thessalonians 3:1) is the request of the apostle Paul, whose faith reached to the possibilities of prayer for the preached Word. The gospel moves altogether too slowly, often timidly, and with feeble steps. What will make this gospel go rapidly like a race runner? What will give this gospel divine effulgence and glory, and cause it to move worthy of God and of Christ? The answer is at hand.

Prayer, more prayer, better prayer will do the deed. This means of grace will give fast going, splendor, and divinity to the gospel.

The possibilities of prayer reach to all things. Whatever concerns man's highest welfare, and whatever has to do with God's plans and purposes concerning men on earth, is a subject for prayer. In "whatever you ask" (John 14:13) is embraced all that concerns us or the children of men and God. And whatever is left out of "whatever" is left out of prayer. Where will we draw the lines which leave out or which will limit the word "whatever"? Define it, and search out and publish the things which the word does not include. If "whatever" does not include all things, then add to it the word "anything." "If you ask anything in My name, I will do it" (John 14:14).

What riches of grace, what blessings, spiritual and temporal, what good for time and eternity, would have been ours had we learned the possibilities of prayer and our faith had taken in the wide range of the divine promises to us to answer prayer! What blessings on our times and what furtherance to God's cause, had we but learned how to pray with large expectations! Who will rise up in this generation and teach the Church this lesson? It is a child's lesson in simplicity, but who has learned it well enough to put prayer to the test? It is a great lesson in its matchless and universal good. The possibilities of prayer are unspeakable, but the lesson of prayer which realizes and measures up to these possibilities, who has learned?

In His discourse in the fifteenth chapter of John, our Lord seems to connect friendship with Him to prayer, and His choosing of His disciples seems to have been with a design that through prayer they should bear much fruit. He said, "You are My friends if you do whatever I command you. . . . You did not choose Me, but I chose you and appointed you that you should go and bear fruit, and that your fruit should remain, that whatever you ask the Father in My name He may give you" (John 15:14, 16).

Here we have again the undefined and unlimited word, "whatsoever," as covering the rights and the things for which we are to pray in the possibilities of prayer.

We have still another declaration from Jesus: "Most assuredly, I say to you, whatever you ask the Father in My name He will give you. Until now you have asked nothing in My name. Ask, and you will receive, that your joy may be full" (John 16:23–24).

Here is a very definite exhortation from our Lord to largeness in praying. Here we are definitely urged by Him to ask for large things; announced with the dignity and solemnity indicated by the solemn phrase, "most assuredly." Why these marvelous urgencies in this last recorded and vital conversation of our Lord with His disciples? The answer is that our Lord might prepare them for the new dispensation, in which prayer was to have such marvelous results, and in which prayer was to be the chief agency to conserve and make aggressive His gospel.

In our Lord's language to His disciples about choosing them that should bear fruit, in this affluent statement of our Lord, He clearly teaches us that this matter of praying and fruit-bearing is not a petty business of our choice or a secondary matter in relation to other matters, but that He has chosen us for this very business of praying. He had specially in mind our praying, and He has chosen us of His own divine selection, and He expects us to do this one thing of praying and to do it intelligently and well.

For He before says that He had made us His friends and had brought us into bosom confidence with Him, and also into free and full conference with Him. The main object of choosing us as His disciples and of friendship with Him was that we might be the better fitted to bear the fruit of prayer.

Let us not forget that we are noting the possibilities of the true praying ones. "Anything" is the word of area and circumference. How far it reaches we may not know. How wide it spreads, our minds fail to discover.

What is there which is not within its reach? Why does Jesus repeat and exhaust these words, all-inclusive and boundless words, if He does not desire to emphasize the unbounded magnificence and illimitable munificence of prayer? Why does He press men to pray, so that our very poverty might be enriched and our limitless inheritance by prayer be secured?

We affirm with absolute certainty that Almighty God answers prayer. The vast possibilities and the urgent necessity of prayer lie in this stupendous fact that God hears and answers prayer. And God hears and answers all prayer. He hears and answers every prayer, where the true conditions of praying are met. Either this is so or it is not. If not, then there is nothing in prayer. Then prayer is but the recitation of words, a mere verbal performance, an empty ceremony. Then prayer is an altogether useless exercise.

But if what we have said is true, then there are vast possibilities in prayer. Then is it far-reaching in its scope, and wide is its range. Then is it true that prayer can lay its hand upon

Almighty God and move Him to do great and wonderful things.

The benefits, the possibilities, and the necessity of prayer are not merely subjective but are peculiarly objective in their character. Prayer aims at a definite object. Prayer has a direct design in view.

Prayer always has something specific before the mind's eye. There may be some subjective benefits which accrue from praying, but this is altogether secondary and incidental.

Prayer always drives directly at an object and seeks to secure a desired end. Prayer is asking, seeking, and knocking at a door for something we have not, which we desire, and which God has promised to us.

Prayer is a direct address to God. "In everything. . .let your requests be made known to God" (Philippians 4:6). Prayer secures blessings and makes men better because it reaches the ear of God. Prayer is only for the betterment of men when it has affected God and moved Him to do something for men. Prayer affects men by affecting God.

Prayer moves men because it moves God to move men. Prayer influences men by influencing God to influence them. Prayer moves the hand that moves the world.

That power is prayer, which soars on high.
Through Jesus to the throne;
And moves the hand which moves the world,
To bring salavation down.

The utmost possibilities of prayer have rarely been realized. The promises of God are so great to those who truly pray, when He puts Himself so fully into the hands of the praying ones, that it almost staggers our faith and causes us to hesitate with astonishment. His promise to answer, and to do and to give "all things," "anything," "whatever," and "all things whatsoever," is so large, so great, so exceedingly broad, that we stand back in amazement and give ourselves to questioning and doubt. We "stagger at the promises through unbelief." Really, the promises of God through prayer have been pared down by us to our little faith and have been brought down to the low level of our narrow notions about God's ability, liberality, and resources. Let us ever keep in mind and never for one moment allow ourselves to doubt the statement that God means what He says in all of His promises. God's promises are His own word. His veracity is at stake in them. To question them is to doubt His veracity. He cannot afford to prove faithless to His word. "In hope of eternal life which God, who cannot lie, promised before time began" (Titus 1:2). His promises are for plain people, and He means to do for all who pray just what He says He will do—"for He who promised is faithful" (Hebrews 10:23).

Unfortunately, we have failed to lay ourselves out in praying. We have limited the Holy One of Israel. The ability to pray can be secured by the grace and power of the Holy Spirit, but it demands so strenuous and high a character that it is a rare thing for a man or woman to be on praying ground and on pleading terms with God. It is as true today as it was in the days of Elijah that "the effective, fervent prayer of a righteous man avails much" (James 5:16). How much such a prayer avails, who can tell?

The possibilities of prayer are the possibilities of faith. Prayer and faith are Siamese twins. One heart animates them both. Faith is always praying. Prayer is always believing. Faith must have a tongue by which it can speak. Prayer is the tongue of faith. Faith must receive. Prayer is the hand of faith stretched out to receive. Prayer must rise and soar. Faith must give prayer the wings to fly and soar. Prayer must have an audience with God. Faith opens the door, and access and audience are given. Prayer asks. Faith lays its hand on the thing asked for.

God's omnipotent power is the basis of omnipotent faith and omnipotent praying. "All things are possible to him who believes" (Mark 9:23), and "whatever things you ask" (Matthew 21:22) are given to him who prays. God's decree and death yield readily to Hezekiah's faith and prayer. When God's promise and man's praying are united by faith, then nothing shall be impossible. Importunate prayer is so all-powerful and irresistible

21

that it obtains promises, or wins where the prospect and the promise seem to be against it. In fact, the New Testament promise includes all things in heaven and in earth. God, by promise, puts all things He possesses into man's hands. Prayer and faith put man in possession of this boundless inheritance.

Prayer is not an indifferent or a small thing. It is not a sweet little privilege. It is a great prerogative, far-reaching in its effects. Failure to pray entails losses far beyond the person who neglects it. Prayer is not a mere episode of the Christian life. Rather, the whole of life is a preparation for and the result of prayer. In its condition, prayer is the sum of religion. Faith is but a channel of prayer. Faith gives it wings and swiftness. Prayer is the lungs through which holiness breathes. Prayer is not only the language of spiritual life, but makes its very essence and forms its real character.

O for a faith that will not shrink
Though pressed by every foe;
That will not tremble on the brink of an earthly woe.
Lord, give us such a faith as this,
And then, whatever may come
We'll tastle even here, this hallowed bliss
Of our eternal home.

2.
THE SECRET OF POWER IN PRAYER
CHARLES H. SPURGEON

"If you abide in Me,
and My words abide in you,
you will ask what you desire,
and it shall be done for you."
JOHN 15:7

Believers do not enjoy the gifts of divine grace all at once. Coming to Christ, we are saved by a true union with Him. But it is by *abiding* in that union that we further receive the purity, the joy, the power, and the blessedness that are stored up in Him for His people. See how our Lord states this when He speaks to the believing Jews in the eighth chapter of this gospel: "If you abide in My word, you are My disciples indeed. And you shall know the truth, and the truth shall make you free" (John 8:31–32). We do not know all the truth of God at once; we learn it by *abiding* in Jesus.

Perseverance in divine grace is an educational process by which we learn the truth of God fully. The emancipating power of that truth is also gradually perceived and enjoyed. The truth will make you free; one bond after another snaps, and we are free indeed. You who are young beginners in the divine life may be cheered to know that there is something better, still, for you—you have not yet received the full recompense of your faith. As our hymn puts it, "It is better than before." You will have happier views of heavenly things as you climb the hill of spiritual experience.

As you abide in Christ, you will have firmer confidence, richer joy, greater stability, more communion with Jesus, and greater delight in the Lord your God.

Infancy is beset with many evils from which manhood is exempt—it is the same in the spiritual as in the natural world.

There are these degrees of attainment among believers, and the Savior here incites us to reach a high position by mentioning a certain privilege that is not for all who say that they are in Christ but for those only who are *abiders* in Him. Every believer should be an abider, but many have hardly earned the name as yet. Jesus says, "If you abide in Me, and My words abide in you, you will ask what you desire, and it shall be done for you" (John 15:7). You have to *live* with Christ to know Him, and the longer you live with Him, the more you will admire and adore Him, and the more you will receive from Him, even grace for grace.

Truly He is a blessed Christ to one who is but a month old in divine grace. But these babes can hardly tell what a precious Jesus He is to those whose acquaintance with Him covers well near half a century! Jesus, in the esteem of abiding believers, grows sweeter and dearer, fairer and lovelier each day. Not that He improves in Himself, for He is perfect. But as *we* increase in our knowledge of Him, we appreciate more thoroughly His matchless excellences.

How glowingly do His old acquaintances exclaim, "Yes, He is altogether lovely!" Oh, that we may continue to grow up in Him in all things who is our head, that we thus may prize Him more and more!

I call your earnest attention to our text, begging you to consider with me three questions. First, what is this special blessing? "You will ask what you desire, and it shall be done for you." Secondly, how is this special blessing obtained? "If you abide in Me, and My words abide in you." Then, thirdly, why is it obtained in this way? There must be a reason for the conditions laid down as necessary to obtaining the promised power in prayer.

Oh, that the anointing of the Holy Spirit that abides on us may now make this subject very profitable to us!

What is this special blessing? Let us read the verse again. Jesus says, "If you abide in Me and My words abide in you, you will ask what you desire, and it shall be done for you."

Observe that our Lord had been warning us that, severed from Him, we can do nothing, and therefore we might naturally have expected that He would now show us how we can do all spiritual acts.

But the text does not run as we should have expected it to run. The Lord Jesus does not say, "Without Me you can do nothing, but if you abide in Me and My words abide in you, you will do all spiritual and gracious things." He does not now speak of what they should, *themselves*, be enabled to do but of what should be done for them.

He says not, "Strength will be given you sufficient for all those holy doings of which you are incapable apart from Me." That would have been true enough, and it is the truth of God that we looked for here. But our most wise Lord improves upon all parallelisms of speech and improves upon all expectancies of heart and says something better still. He does not say, "If you abide in Me and My words abide in you, you will do spiritual things." But, "*you will ask.*" By prayer you will be enabled to do. But before all attempts to do, you will ask. The choice privilege here given is a mighty prevailing *prayerfulness*. Power in prayer is very much the gauge of our spiritual condition. And when that is secured to us in a high degree, we are favored as to all other matters.

One of the first results, then, of our abiding union with Christ will be the certain exercise of prayer. You will ask. If others neither seek, nor knock, nor ask, you, at any rate, will do so. Those who keep away from Jesus do not pray. Those in whom communion with Christ is suspended feel as if they could not pray. But Jesus says, "If you abide in Me, and My words abide in you, you will ask." Prayer comes spontaneously from those who abide in Jesus, even as certain oriental trees, without pressure, shed their fragrant gums.

Prayer is the natural out-gushing of a soul in communion with Jesus. Just as the leaf and the fruit will come out of the vine without any conscious effort on the part of the branch but simply because of its living union with the stem, so prayer buds and blossoms and produces fruit out of souls abiding in Jesus. As stars shine, so do abiders pray. It is their use and their second nature. They do not say to themselves, "Now it is the time for us to get to our task and pray." No, they pray as wise men eat, namely, when the desire for it is upon them. They do not cry out as under bondage, "At this time I ought to be in prayer but I do not feel like it. What a weariness it is!" No, they have a glad errand at the mercy seat and they are rejoiced to go upon it.

Hearts abiding in Christ send forth supplications as fires send out flames and sparks. Souls abiding in Jesus open the day with prayer. Prayer surrounds them as an atmosphere all day long. At night they fall asleep praying. I have known them even to dream a prayer and, at any rate, they are able joyfully to say, "When I awake, I am still with You." Habitual asking comes out of abiding in Christ. You will not need urging to pray when you are abiding with Jesus. He says you will ask. And depend upon it, you will!

You will also feel most powerfully the *necessity* of prayer. Your great need of prayer will be vividly seen. Do I hear you say, "What? When we abide in Christ and His words abide in us, have we not already attained?" Far are we, then, from being satisfied with ourselves. It is *then* that we feel more than ever that we must ask for *more* divine grace. He that knows Christ best knows his own necessities best.

He that is most conscious of life in Christ is also most convinced of his own death apart from Christ. He who most clearly discerns the perfect character of Jesus will be most urgent in prayer for divine grace to grow like He. The more I seem to be in my Lord, the more I desire to obtain from Him, since I know that all that is in Him is put there on purpose that I may receive it.

"Of His fullness we have all received, and grace for grace" (John 1:16). It is just in proportion as we are linked to Christ's fullness that we feel the necessity of drawing from it by constant prayer.

Nobody needs to prove to an abider in Christ the doctrine of prayer, for we enjoy the thing itself. Prayer is now as much a necessity of our spiritual life as breath is of our natural life—we cannot live without asking favors of the Lord! "If you abide in Me, and My words abide in you, you will ask"—and you will not wish to cease from asking. He has said, "Seek My face," and your heart will answer, "Your face, LORD, I will seek" (Psalm 27:8).

Note next, that the fruit of our abiding is not only the exercise of prayer and a sense of the necessity of prayer, but it includes *liberty* in prayer. "You will ask what you desire." Have you not been on your knees at times without power to pray? Have you not felt that you could not plead as you desired? You wanted to pray but the waters were frozen up and would not flow. You said mournfully, "I am shut up, and I cannot get out" (Psalm 88:8). The will was present but not the freedom to present that will in prayer. Do you, then, desire liberty in prayer so that you may speak with God as a man speaks with his friend? Here is the way to it, "If you abide in Me, and My words abide in you, you will ask what you desire."

I do not mean that you will gain liberty as to mere fluency of utterance—for that is a very *inferior* gift. Fluency is a questionable endowment, especially when it is not attended with weight of thought and depth of feeling. Some brethren pray by the yard.

But true prayer is measured by weight and not by length. A single groan before God may have more fullness of prayer in it than a fine oration of great length. He that dwells with God in Christ Jesus is the man whose steps are enlarged in intercession.

He comes boldly because he abides at the throne. He sees the golden scepter stretched out and hears the King saying, "Ask what you will and it will be done to you."

It is the man who abides in conscious union with his Lord who has freedom of access in prayer. Well may he come to Christ readily, for he is in Christ, and abides in Him. Attempt not to seize this holy liberty by excitement, or presumption—there is but one way of really gaining it and here it is—"If you abide in Me, and My words abide in you, you will ask what you desire." By this means alone will you be enabled to open your mouth wide, that God may fill it. Thus will you become Israel's children, and as princes, have power with God.

This is not all. The favored man has the privilege of successful prayer. "You will ask what you desire, and it shall be done for you." You may not do it, but it will be done to you. You long to bear fruit. Ask and it will be done to you. Look at the vine branch. It simply remains in the vine, and by remaining in the vine, the fruit comes from it. It is done to it. Brothers and sisters in Christ, the purpose of your being, its one object and design, is to bring forth fruit to the glory of the Father. To gain this end you must abide in Christ, as the branch abides in the vine. This is the method by which your prayer for fruitfulness will become successful. "It shall be done for you."

Concerning this matter, "you will ask what you desire, and it shall be done for you." You will have wonderful prevalence with God in prayer, insomuch that before you call, He will answer, and while you are yet speaking, He will hear. "The desire of the righteous will be granted" (Proverbs 10:24). To the same effect is the other text: "Delight yourself also in the LORD, and He shall give you the desires of your heart" (Psalm

37:4). There is a great breadth in this text, "You will ask what you desire, and it shall be done for you." The Lord gives the abider carte blanche. He puts into his hand a signed check and permits him to fill it up as he wills.

Does the text mean what it says? I never knew my Lord to say anything He did not mean. I am sure that He may sometimes mean more than we understand Him to say, but He never means less. Mind you, He does not say to all men, "I will give you whatever you ask." Oh no, that would be an unkind kindness— but He speaks to His disciples and says, "If you abide in Me, and My words abide in you, you will ask what you desire, and it shall be done for you." It is to a certain class of men who have already received great grace at His hands.

It is to them He commits this marvelous power of prayer.

O my dear friends, if I may covet earnestly one thing above every other, it is that I may be able to ask what I will of the Lord and have it! The man who prevails in prayer is the man to preach successfully, for he may well prevail with man for God when he has already prevailed with God for men! This is the man to face the difficulties of business life. For what can baffle him when he can take all to God in prayer? One such man as this, or one such woman as this in a church is worth ten thousand of us common people. In these we find the peerage of the skies. In these are the men in whom is fulfilled God's purpose concerning man, whom He made to have dominion over all the works of His hands.

The stamp of sovereignty is on the brows of these men. They shape the history of nations, they guide the current events through their power on high. We see Jesus with all things put under Him by the divine purpose, and as we rise into that image, we also are clothed with dominion and are made kings and priests to God.

Behold Elijah, with the keys of the rain swinging at his girdle, he shuts or opens the windows of heaven! There are such men still alive. Aspire to be such men and women,

I beseech you, that to you the text may be fulfilled, "You will ask what you desire, and it shall be done for you."

The text seems to imply that if we reach this point of privilege, this gift will be a perpetuity. "You will ask," you will always ask; you will never get beyond asking, but you will ask successfully. "You will ask what you desire, and it shall be done for you." Here we have the gift of *continual* prayer.

Not for the week of prayer, not during a month's conference, nor upon a few special occasions will you pray prevailingly. But you will possess this power with God so long as you abide in Christ and His words abide in you. God will put His omnipotence at your disposal. He will put forth His Godhead to fulfill the desires that His own Spirit has worked in you.

I wish I could make this jewel glitter before the eyes of all the saints till they cried out, "Oh, that we had it!" This power in prayer is like the sword of Goliath. Wisely may every David say, "There is none like it; give it to me"

(1 Samuel 21:9). This weapon of all-prayer beats the enemy and at the same time enriches its possessor with all the wealth of God. How can he lack anything to whom the Lord has said, "Ask what you will, and it will be done to you?" Oh come, let us seek this promise. Listen and learn the way. Follow me, while by the light of the text I point out the path. May the Lord lead us in it by His Holy Spirit!

3.
ON PRAYER AND THE PRINCIPAL EXERCISES OF PIETY
FRANÇOIS FÉNELON AND MADAME JEANNE GUYON

*We do not know what we should pray
for as we ought, but the Spirit Himself
makes intercession for us with
groanings which cannot be uttered.*
ROMANS 8:26

True prayer is only another name for the love of God. Its excellence does not consist in the multitude of our words; for our Father knows what things we have need of before we ask Him. The true prayer is that of the heart, and the heart prays only for what it desires. To pray, then, is to desire—but to desire what God would have us desire. He who asks what he does, not from the bottom of his heart's desire, is mistaken in thinking that he prays. Let him spend days in reciting prayers, in meditation, or in inciting himself to pious exercises—he prays not once truly, if he really doesn't desire the things he pretends to ask.

How few there are who pray—for how few are they who desire what is truly good! Crosses, external and internal humiliation, renouncement of our own wills, the death of self, and the establishment of God's throne upon the ruins of self-love—these are indeed good; not to desire these, is not to pray; to desire them seriously, soberly, constantly, and with reference to all the details of life, this is true prayer; not to desire them, and yet to suppose we pray, is an illusion like that of the wretched who dream themselves happy. Alas! how many souls full of self, and of an imaginary desire for perfection in the midst of hosts of voluntary imperfections, have never yet uttered this true prayer of the heart! It is in reference to this that St. Augustine says: "He that loveth little, prayeth little; he that loveth much, prayeth much."

On the other hand, that heart in which the true love of God and true desire exist never ceases to pray. Love, hidden in the bottom of the soul, prays without ceasing, even when the mind is drawn another way. God continually beholds the desire which He has Himself implanted in the soul, though it may at times be unconscious of its existence; His heart is touched by it; it ceaselessly attracts His mercies; it is that Spirit which, according to St. Paul, helps our infirmities and "makes intercession for us with groanings which cannot be uttered" (Romans 8:26).

Love desires of God that He would give us what we need and that He would have less regard to our frailty than to the purity of our intentions. It even covers over our trifling defects and purifies us like a consuming fire: "He makes intercession for the saints according to the will of God" (Romans 8:27). For "we do not know what we should pray for as we ought" (Romans 8:26) and, in our ignorance, frequently request what would be injurious; we should like fervor of devotion, distinct sensible joys, and apparent perfections, which would serve to nourish within us the life of self and a confidence in our own strength; but love leads us on, abandons us to all the operations of grace, puts us entirely at the disposal of God's will, and thus prepares us for all His secret designs.

Then we will all things and yet nothing. What God gives is precisely what we should have desired to ask; for we will whatever He wills and only that. Thus, this state contains all prayer: it is a work of the heart which includes all desire. The Spirit prays within us for those very things which the Spirit Himself wills to give us.

Even when we are occupied with outward things, and our thoughts drawn off by the providential engagements of our position, we still carry within us a constantly burning fire, which not only cannot be extinguished but nourishes a secret prayer, and is like a lamp continually lighted before the throne of God, "I sleep, but my heart is awake" (Song of Solomon 5:2). "Blessed are those servants whom the master, when he comes, will find watching" (Luke 12:37).

There are two principal points of attention

necessary for the preservation of this constant spirit of prayer which unites us with God: We must continually seek to cherish it, and we must avoid everything that tends to make us lose it.

In order to cherish it, we should pursue a regulated course of reading; we must have appointed seasons of secret prayer, and frequent states of recollection during the day; we should make use of retirement when we feel the need of it, or when it is advised by those of greater experience, and unite in the ordinances appropriate to our condition.

We should greatly fear and be exceedingly cautious to avoid all things that have a tendency to make us lose this state of prayer. Thus we should decline those worldly occupations and associates which dissipate the mind, pleasures which excite the passions, and everything calculated to awaken the love of the world and those old inclinations that have caused us so much trouble.

There is an infinity of detail in these two heads; general directions only can be given, because each individual case presents features peculiar to itself.

We should choose those works for reading which instruct us in our duty and in our faults; which, while they point out the greatness of God, teach us what is our duty to Him, and how very far we are from performing it; not those barren productions which melt and sentimentalize the heart; *the tree must bear fruit*; we can only judge of the life of the root by its fecundity.

The first effect of a sincere love is an earnest desire to know all that we ought to do to gratify the object of our affection.

Any other desire is a proof that we love ourselves under a pretense of loving God; that we are seeking an empty and deceitful consolation in Him; that we would use God as an instrument for our pleasure, instead of sacrificing that for His glory. God forbid that His children should so love Him! Cost what it may, we must both know and do without reservation what He requires of us.

Seasons of secret prayer must be regulated

by the leisure, the disposition, the condition, and the inward impulse of each individual.

Meditation is not prayer, but it is its necessary foundation; it brings to mind the truths which God has revealed. We should be conversant not only with all the mysteries of Jesus Christ, and the truths of His gospel, but also with everything they ought to operate in us for our regeneration; we should be colored and penetrated by them as wool is by the dye.

So familiar should they become to us, that, in consequence of seeing them at all times and ever near to us, we may acquire the habit of forming no judgment except in their light; that they may be to us our only guide in matters of practice, as the rays of the sun are our only light in matters of perception.

When these truths are once, as it were, incorporated in us, then it is that our praying begins to be real and fruitful. Up to that point it was but the shadow; we thought we had penetrated to the inmost recesses of the gospel, when we had barely set foot upon the vestibule—all our most tender and lively feelings, all our firmest resolutions, all our clearest and farthest views, were but the rough and shapeless mass from which God would hew in us His likeness.

When His celestial rays begin to shine within us, then we see in the true light; then there is no truth to which we do not instantaneously assent, as we admit, without any process of reasoning, the splendor of the sun, the moment we behold His rising beams. Our union with God must be the result of our faithfulness in doing and suffering all His will.

Our meditations should become every day deeper and more interior. I say *deeper*, because by frequent and humble meditation upon God's truth, we penetrate further and further in search of new treasures; and *more interior*, because as we sink more and more to enter into these truths, they also descend to penetrate the very substance of our souls. Then it is that a simple word goes further than whole sermons.

The very things which had been fruitlessly

and coldly heard a hundred times before, now nourish the soul with a hidden manna, having an infinite variety of flavors for days in succession. Let us beware, too, of ceasing to meditate upon truths which have heretofore been blessed to us, so long as there remains any nourishment in them, so long as they yet yield us anything; it is a certain sign that we still need their ministration; we derive instruction from them without receiving any precise or distinct impression; there is an indescribable something in them, which helps us more than all our reasonings. We behold a truth, we love it and repose upon it; it strengthens the soul and detaches us from ourselves; let us dwell upon it in peace as long as possible.

As to the manner of meditating, it should not be subtle, nor composed of long reasonings; simple and natural reflections derived immediately from the subject of our thoughts are all that is required.

We need take a few truths; meditate upon these without hurry, without effort, and without seeking for far-fetched reflections.

Every truth should be considered with reference to its practical bearing. To receive it without employing all means to put it faithfully in practice at whatever cost, is to "suppress the truth in unrighteousness" (Romans 1:18); it is a resistance to the truth impressed upon us, and of course, to the Holy Spirit. This is the most terrible of all unfaithfulness.

As to a method in prayer, each one must be guided by his own experience.

Those who find themselves profited in using a strict method need not depart from it, while those who cannot so confine themselves may make use of their own mode, without ceasing to respect that which has been useful to many, and which so many pious and experienced persons have highly recommended. A method is intended to assist; if it be found to embarrass instead of assist, the sooner it is discarded the better.

The most natural mode, at first, is to take a book, and to cease reading whenever we feel so inclined by the passage upon which we are engaged, and, whenever that no longer ministers to our interior nourishment, to begin again. As a general rule, those truths which we highly relish and which shed a degree of practical light upon the things which we are required to give up for God, are leadings of divine grace, which we should follow without hesitation. "The wind blows where it wishes" (John 3:8), and "Where the Spirit of the Lord is, there is liberty" (2 Corinthians 3:17).

In the course of time the proportion of reflections and reasonings will diminish, and that of tender feelings, affecting views and desires, will increase as we become sufficiently instructed and convinced by the Holy Spirit. The heart is satisfied, nourished, warmed, set on fire; a word only will give it employment for a long time.

Finally, increase of prayer is indicated by an increase of simplicity and steadiness in our views, a great multitude of objects and considerations being no longer necessary. Our intercourse with God resembles that with a friend; at first, there are a thousand things to be told and as many to be asked; but after a time, these diminish, while the pleasure of being together does not. Everything has been said, but the satisfaction of seeing each other, of feeling that one is near the other, or reposing in the enjoyment of a pure and sweet friendship, can be felt without conversation; the silence is eloquent and mutually understood. Each feels that the other is in perfect sympathy with him and that their two hearts are incessantly poured one into the other, and constitute but one.

Thus it is that in prayer, our communion with God becomes a simple and familiar union, far beyond the need of words. But let it be remembered that God Himself must alone institute this prayer within us; nothing would be more rash nor more dangerous than to dare to attempt it of ourselves.

We must suffer ourselves to be led step by step, by someone conversant with the ways of God, who may lay the immovable foundations of correct teaching, and of the complete death of self in everything.

Our leisure and our needs must regulate our retirements; *our needs,* because it is with the soul as with the body; when we can no longer work without nourishment, we must take it; we shall otherwise be in danger of fainting. *Our leisure*, because, this absolute necessity of food excepted, we must attend to duty before we seek enjoyment in spiritual exercises. The man who has public duties and spends the time appropriate to them in meditating in retirement, would miss of God while he was seeking to be united to Him.

True union with God is to do His will without ceasing, in spite of all our natural disinclination and in every duty of life, however disagreeable or mortifying.

As precautions against wanderings, we must avoid close and intimate intercourse with those who are not pious, especially when we have been before led astray by their infectious maxims. They will open our wounds afresh; they have a secret correspondence deep in our souls; there resides a soft and insinuating counselor who is always ready to blind and deceive us.

Would you judge of a man? Observe who

are his companions. How can he who loves God, and who loves nothing except in and for God, enjoy the intimate companionship of those who neither love nor know God, and who look upon love to Him as a weakness? Can a heart full of God and sensible of its own frailty ever rest and be at ease with those who have no feelings in common with it, but who are ever seeking to rob it of its treasure? Their delights, and the pleasures of which Faith is the source, are incompatible.

I am well aware that we cannot, nay, that we ought not to break with those friends to whom we are bound by esteem of their natural amiability, by their services, by the tie of sincere friendship, or by the regard consequent upon mutual good offices. Friends whom we have treated with a certain familiarity and confidence would be wounded to the quick were we to separate from them entirely; we must gently and imperceptibly diminish our itercourse with them without abruptly declaring our alteration of sentiment; we may see them in private, distinguish them from our less intimate friends, and confide to them those matters in which their integrity and friendship enable them to give us good advice, and to think with us, although our reasons for so thinking are more pure and elevated than theirs. In short, we may continue to serve them, and to manifest all the attentions of a cordial friendship, without suffering our hearts to be embarrassed by them.

How perilous is our state without this precaution! If we do not, from the first, boldly adopt all measures to render our piety entirely free and independent of our unregenerate friends, it is threatened with a speedy downfall. If a man surrounded by such companions be of a yielding disposition and inflammable passions, it is certain that his friends, even the best-intentioned ones, will lead him astray.

They may be good, honest, faithful, and possessed of all those qualities which render friendship perfect in the eye of the world; but, for him, they are infected, and their amiability only increases the danger.

Those who have not this estimable character should be sacrificed at once; blessed are we, when a sacrifice that ought to cost us so little may avail to give us so precious a security for our eternal salvation!

Not only, then, should we be exceedingly careful whom we will see, but we must also reserve the necessary time that we may see God alone in prayer. Those who have stations of importance to fill have generally so many indispensable duties to perform that, without the greatest care in the management of their time, none will be left to be alone with God. If they have ever so little inclination for dissipation, the hours that belong to God and their neighbor disappear altogether.

We must be firm in observing our rules. This strictness seems excessive, but without it everything falls into confusion; we become dissipated, relaxed, and lose strength; we insensibly separate from God, surrender ourselves to all our pleasures, and only then begin to perceive that we have wandered, when it is almost hopeless to think of endeavoring to return.

Prayer, prayer! This is our only safety. "Blessed be God, who has not turned away my prayer, nor His mercy from me!" (Psalm 66:20). And to be faithful in prayer, it is indispensable that we should dispose all the employments of the day, with a regularity nothing can disturb.

4.
PRAYER MUST BE SPECIFIC
ANDREW MURRAY

*So Jesus answered and said to him,
"What do you want Me to do for you?"*
MARK 10:51

The blind man had been crying out loudly, and that a great deal, "Son of David, have mercy on me!" (Mark 10:47). The cry had reached the ear of the Lord, and He knew what the man wanted and was ready to grant it to him. But before He does it, He asks him, "What do you want me to do for you?" He wants to hear from the man's own lips, not only the general request for mercy, but the distinct expression of what his desire was. Until he speaks it out, he is not healed.

There is now still many a petitioner to whom the Lord puts the same question, and who cannot, until it is answered, get the aid he asks. Our prayers must not be a vague appeal to His mercy or an indefinite cry for blessing, but a distinct expression of definite need. Not that His loving heart does not understand our cries or is not ready to hear. But He desires it for our own sakes. Such definite prayer teaches us to know our own needs better. It demands time, thought, and self-examination to find out what our greatest need really is.

It searches us and puts us to the test as to whether our desires are honest and real, such as we are ready to persevere in.

It leads us to judge whether our desires are according to God's Word, and whether we really believe we shall receive the things we ask for. It helps us to wait for the specific answer and to recognize it when it comes.

And yet how much of our prayer is vague and pointless. Some cry for mercy, but don't take the trouble to know what mercy must do for them. Others ask, perhaps, to be delivered from sin, but do not begin by bringing any sin by name from which the deliverance can be claimed. Still others pray for God's blessing on those around them, for the outpouring of God's Spirit on their land or on the world, and yet they have no special field where they wait and expect to see the answer. To every one of these the Lord says, "What do you want Me to do for you?"

Every Christian has only limited powers, and just as he must have his own specific field of labor in which he works, so it is with his prayers, too. Each believer has his own circle: family, friends, and neighbors. If he were to take one or more of these by name, he would find this really brings him into the training school of faith, which leads to personal and pointed dealing with his God. It is when in such distinct matters we have in faith claimed and received answers that our more general prayers will be believing and effective.

We all know with what surprise the whole civilized world heard of the way in which trained troops were repulsed by the Transvaal Boers at Majuba. And to what did they owe their success? In the armies of Europe, the solider fires on the enemy standing in large masses, and never thinks of seeking an aim for every bullet.

In hunting game, the Boer had learned a

different lesson: his practiced eye knew to send every bullet on its special mission, to seek and find its man. Such aiming must gain the day in the spiritual world, too.

As long as in prayer we just pour out our hearts in a multitude of petitions without taking time to see whether every petition is sent with the purpose and expectation of getting an answer, not many will reach the mark. But if, as in silence of the soul we bow before the Lord, we were ready to answer questions such as these: What is now really my desire? Do I desire it in faith, expecting to receive? Am I now ready to place and leave it there in the Father's bosom? Is it settled between God and me that I am to have the answer?—we should learn to pray in such a way that God will see and we would know what we really expect.

It is for this reason, among others, that the Lord warns us against the vain repetitions of the Gentiles, who expect to be heard because they pray so much (see Matthew 6:7–8). We often hear prayers of great earnestness and fervor, in which a multitude of petitions are poured forth, but to which the Savior would undoubtedly answer, "What do you want Me to do for you?"

If I am in a strange land, in the interests of the business my father owns, I would certainly write two different sorts of letters home. There will be family letters giving expression to the interaction to which affection prompts, and there will be business letters containing orders for what I need. There may also be letters in which both are found. The answers will correspond to the letters. To each sentence of the letters containing the family news, I do not expect a special answer. But for each order I send, I am confident of an answer as to whether the desired article has been sent. In our dealings with God, the business element must not be lacking.

With our expressions of need and sin, of love and faith and consecration, there must be the specific statement of what we ask and expect to receive. It is in the answer that the Father loves to give us a proof of His approval and acceptance.

But the word of the Master teaches us

more. He does not say, "What do you *wish*?" but "What do you *want*?" One often wishes for a thing without willing it.

I wish to have a certain item, but I find the price is too high, so I decide not to take it. I *wish* but do not *will* to have it. The lazy man wishes to be rich, but does not will it. Many a man wishes to be saved, but perishes because he does not will it. The will rules the whole heart and life. If I really will to have something that is within my reach, I do not rest until I have it. When Jesus asks us, "What do you want?" He asks whether it is indeed our purpose to have what we ask for at any price, however great the sacrifice. Do you really will to have it enough that, though He waits to answer, you will not hold your peace until He hears you? Sadly, many prayers are wishes sent up for a short time and then forgotten, or sent up year after year as a matter of duty, while we remain content with the prayer without the answer.

But, it may be asked, is it not best to make our wishes known to God and then leave it to Him to decide what is best, without our seeking to assert our will? By no means! This is the very essence of the prayer of faith to which Jesus sought to train His disciples, that it does not only make known its desire and then leave the decision to God. That would be the prayer of submission for cases in which we cannot know God's will. But the prayer of faith, finding God's will in some promise of the Word, pleads for that until it comes.

In Matthew 9:28, we read that Jesus said to the blind man, "*Do you believe* that I am able to do this?" In Mark He said, "*What do you want* Me to do for you?" (10:51). In both cases, He said that faith had saved them. And He said to the Syrophoenician woman, too, "Great is your faith! Let it be to you as you desire" (Matthew 15:28). Faith is nothing but the purpose of the will resting on God's Word and saying, "I must have it." To believe truly is to will firmly.

But is not such a will at odds with our dependence on God and our submission to Him? By no means! Rather, it is the true submission that honors God. It is only when the child has yielded his own will in entire surrender to the Father that he receives from the Father the liberty and power to will what he desires. But once the believer has accepted the will of God, as revealed through the Word and the Spirit, as his will, too, then it is the will of God that His child should use this renewed will in His service. The will is the highest power of the soul. Grace wants above everything to sanctify and restore this will, one of the chief traits of God's image, to full and free exercise. As a son who lives only for his father's interests, who seeks not his own but his father's will, is trusted by the father with his business, so God speaks to His child in all truth, "What do you want?"

It is often spiritual complacency that, under the appearance of humility, professes to have no will because it fears the trouble of searching for the will of God, or, when that will is found, the struggle of claiming it in faith. True humility is always accompanied by strong faith, which only seeks to know what is according to the will of God and then boldly claims the fulfillment of the promise: "You will ask what you desire, and it shall be done for you" (John 15:7).

"LORD, TEACH US TO PRAY."

Lord Jesus! Teach me to pray with all my heart and strength so that there may be no doubt with You or with me about what I have asked. May I know so well what I desire that, even as my requests are recorded in heaven, I can also record them on earth and note each answer as it comes. And may my faith in what Your Word has promised be so clear that the Spirit may indeed work within me the liberty to will that it will come. Lord! Renew, strengthen, and sanctify wholly my will for the work of effectual prayer.

Blessed Savior! I pray that You will reveal to me the wonderful grace You show us, thus asking us to say what we desire that You should do, and promising to do whatever we desire. Son of God! I cannot fully understand it. I can only believe that You have, indeed, redeemed us wholly for Yourself, and that You seek to make the will, as our noblest part, Your most effective servant. Lord! I most unreservedly yield my will to You as the power through which Your Spirit is to rule my whole being. Let Him take possession of it, lead it into the truth of Your promises, and make it so strong in prayer that I may always hear Your voice saying, "Great is your faith! Let it be to you as you desire." Amen.

5.
Hindrances to Prayer
R. A. Torrey

You ask and do not receive,
because you ask amiss.
James 4:3

We have gone very carefully into the positive conditions of prevailing prayer; but there are some things which hinder prayer. These God has made very plain in His Word.

The first hindrance to prayer we will find in James 4:3, "You ask and do not receive, because you ask amiss, that you may spend it on your pleasures."

A selfish purpose in prayer robs prayer of power. Very many prayers are selfish.

These may be prayers for things for which it is perfectly proper to ask, for things which it is the will of God to give, but the motive of the prayer is entirely wrong, and so the prayer falls powerless to the ground. The true purpose in prayer is that God may be glorified in the answer.

If we ask any petition merely that we may

receive something to use in our pleasures or in our own gratification in one way or another, we "ask amiss" and need not expect to receive what we ask.

This explains why many prayers remain unanswered.

For example, many a woman is praying for the conversion of her husband.

That certainly is a most proper thing to ask; but many a woman's motive in asking for the conversion of her husband is entirely improper; it is selfish. She desires that her husband may be converted because it would be so much more pleasant for her to have a husband who sympathized with her; or it is so painful to think that her husband might die and be lost forever. For some such selfish reason as this, she desires to have her husband converted. The prayer is purely selfish. Why should a woman desire the conversion of her husband? First of all and above all, that God may be glorified; because she cannot bear the thought that God the Father should be dishonored by her husband trampling underfoot the Son of God.

Many pray for a revival. That certainly is a prayer that is pleasing to God; it is along the line of His will; but many prayers for revivals are purely selfish. The churches desire revivals in order that the membership may be increased, in order that the church may have a position of more power and influence in the community, in order that the church treasury may be filled, in order that a good report may be made at the presbytery or conference or association.

For such low purposes as these churches and ministers oftentimes pray for a revival, and oftentimes, too, God does not answer the prayer. Why should we pray for a revival? For the glory of God, because we cannot endure it that God should continue to be dishonored by the worldliness of the church, by the sins of unbelievers, by the proud unbelief of the day; because God's Word is being made void; in order that God may be glorified by the outpouring of His Spirit on the Church of Christ. For these reasons first of all and above all, we should pray for a revival.

Many a prayer for the Holy Spirit is a purely selfish prayer. It certainly is God's will to give the Holy Spirit to them that ask Him—He has told us so plainly in His Word (Luke 11:13), but many a prayer for the Holy Spirit is hindered by the selfishness of the motive that lies behind the prayer. Men and women pray for the Holy Spirit in order that they may be happy, or in order that they may be saved from the wretchedness of defeat in their lives, or in order that they may have power as Christian workers, or for some other purely selfish motive. Why should we pray for the Spirit? In order that God may no longer be dishonored by the low level of our Christian lives and by our ineffectiveness in service; in order that God may be glorified in the new beauty that comes into our lives and the new power that comes into our service.

The second hindrance to prayer we find in Isaiah 59:1–2: "Behold, the LORD's hand is not shortened, that it cannot save; nor His ear heavy, that it cannot hear. But your iniquities have separated you from your God; and your sins have hidden His face from you, so that He will not hear."

Sin hinders prayer. Many a man prays and prays and prays, and gets absolutely no answer to his prayer. Perhaps he is tempted to think that it is not the will of God to answer, or he may think that the days when God answered prayer, if He ever did, are over. So the Israelites seem to have thought. They thought that the Lord's hand was shortened, that it could not save, and that His ear had become heavy that it could no longer hear.

"Not so," said Isaiah. "God's ear is just as open to hear as ever, His hand just as mighty to save; but there is a hindrance.

"That hindrance is your own sins. Your iniquities have separated you and your God, and your sins have hid His face from you that He will not hear."

It is so today. Many a man is crying to God in vain, simply because of sin in his life. It may be some sin in the past that has been unconfessed and unjudged; it may be some sin in the present that is cherished, very likely is not even looked upon as sin, but there the sin is, hidden away somewhere in the heart or in the life, and God "will not hear" because of it.

Anyone who finds his prayers ineffective should not conclude that the thing which he asks of God is not according to His will, but should go alone with God with the psalmist's prayer, "Search me, O God, and know my heart; try me, and know my anxieties; and see if there is any wicked way in me" (Psalm 139:23–24), and wait before Him until He puts His finger upon the thing that is displeasing in His sight. Then this sin should be confessed and put away.

I well remember a time in my life when

I was praying for two definite things that it seemed that I must have or God would be dishonored; but the answer did not come.

I awoke in the middle of the night in great physical suffering and great distress of soul. I cried to God for these things, reasoned with Him as to how necessary it was that I get them, and get them at once; but no answer came. I asked God to show me if there was anything wrong in my own life. Something came to my mind that had often come to it before, something definite but which I was unwilling to confess as sin. I said to God, "If this is wrong I will give it up," but still no answer came. In my innermost heart, though I had never admitted it, I knew it was wrong.

At last I said: "This is wrong. I have sinned. I will give it up." I found peace. In a few moments I was sleeping like a child.

In the morning I woke well in body, and the money that was so much needed for the honor of God's name came.

Sin is an awful thing, and one of the most awful things about it is the way it hinders prayer, the way it severs the connection between us and the Source of all grace and power and blessing. Anyone who would have power in prayer must be merciless in dealing with his own sins. "If I regard iniquity in my heart, the Lord will not hear" (Psalm 66:18). So long as we hold on to sin or have any controversy with God, we cannot expect Him to heed our prayers.

If there is anything that constantly comes up in your moments of close communion with God, that is the thing that hinders prayer: Put it away.

The third hindrance to prayer is found in Ezekiel 14:3: "Son of man, these men have set up their idols in their hearts, and put before them that which causes them to stumble into iniquity. Should I let Myself be inquired of at all by them?"

Idols in the heart cause God to refuse to listen to our prayers! What is an idol? An idol is anything that takes the place of God, anything that is the supreme object of our affection. God alone has the right to the supreme place in our hearts. Everything and everyone else must be subordinate to Him.

Many a man makes an idol of his wife. Not that a man can love his wife too much, but he can put her in the wrong place, he can put her before God—and when a man regards his wife's pleasure before God's pleasure, when he gives her the first place and

God the second place, his wife is an idol, and God cannot hear his prayers.

Many a woman makes an idol of her children. Not that we can love our children too much. The more dearly we love Christ, the more dearly we love our children; but we can put our children in the wrong place, we can put them before God and their interests before God's interests. When we do this our children are our idols.

Many a man makes an idol of his reputation or his business. When reputation or business is put before God, God cannot hear the prayers of such a man.

One great question for us to decide, if we would have power in prayer, is *Is God absolutely first?* Is He before wife, before children, before reputation, before business, before our own lives? If not, prevailing prayer is impossible.

God often calls our attention to the fact that we have an idol by not answering our prayers. That leads us to inquire as to why our prayers are not answered, and so we discover the idol. When we put it away, God hears our prayers.

The fourth hindrance to prayer is found in Proverbs 21:13: "Whoever shuts his ears to the cry of the poor will also cry himself and not be heard."

There is perhaps no greater hindrance to prayer than stinginess, the lack of liberality toward the poor and toward God's work. It is the one who gives generously to others who receives generously from God.

"Give, and it will be given to you: good measure, pressed down, shaken together, and running over will be put into your bosom. For with the same measure that you use, it will be measured back to you" (Luke 6:38). The generous man is the mighty man of prayer. The stingy man is the powerless man of prayer.

One of the most wonderful statements about prevailing prayer is found in 1 John 3:22, "Whatever we ask we receive from Him, because we keep His commandments and do those things that are pleasing in His sight." This statement is made in direct connection with generosity toward the needy. In the context, we are told that it is when we love, not in word or in tongue but in deed and in truth; when we open our hearts toward the brother in need, it is then and only then that we have confidence toward God in prayer.

Many a man or woman who is seeking to find the secret of their powerlessness in prayer need not seek far; it is nothing more nor less than downright stinginess. George Muller was a mighty man of prayer because he was a mighty giver. What he received from God never stuck to his fingers; he immediately passed it on to others. He was constantly receiving because he was constantly giving. When one thinks of the selfishness of the professing church today, it is no wonder that the church has so little power in prayer. If we would get from God, we must give to others.

Perhaps the most wonderful promise in the Bible in regard to God's supplying our need is found in Philippians 4:19, "And my God shall supply all your need according to His riches in glory by Christ Jesus." This glorious promise was made to the Philippian church in immediate connection with their generosity.

The fifth hindrance to prayer is found in Mark 11:25, "And whenever you stand praying, if you have anything against anyone, forgive him, that your Father in heaven may also forgive you your trespasses."

An unforgiving spirit is one of the most common hindrances to prayer. Prayer is answered on the basis that our sins are forgiven; God cannot deal with us on the basis of forgiveness while we are harboring ill will against those who have wronged us.

Anyone who is nursing a grudge against

another has fast closed the ear of God against his own petition.

How many there are crying to God for the conversion of husband, children, friends—and wondering why it is that their prayers are not answered, when the whole secret is some grudge that they have in their hearts against someone who has injured them, or who they fancy has injured them. Many a mother and father are allowing their children to go down to eternity unsaved, for the miserable gratification of hating someone else.

The sixth hindrance to prayer is found in 1 Peter 3:7, "Husbands, likewise, dwell with [your wives] with understanding, giving honor to the wife, as to the weaker vessel, and as being heirs together of the grace of life, that your prayers may not be hindered."

Here we are plainly told that a wrong relation between husband and wife is a hindrance to prayer. In many a case, the prayers of husbands are hindered because of their failure of duty toward their wives.

On the other hand, it is also doubtless true that the prayers of wives are hindered because of their failure in duty toward their husbands. If husbands and wives should seek diligently to find the cause of their unanswered prayers, they would often find it in their relations to one another.

Many a man who makes great pretentions to piety and is very active in Christian work, shows but little consideration in his treatment of his wife, and is oftentimes unkind, if not brutal; then he wonders why it is that his prayers are not answered. The verse that we have just quoted explains the seeming mystery. On the other hand, many a woman who is very devoted to the church and very faithful in attendance upon all services, treats her husband with the most unpardonable neglect, is cross and peevish toward him, wounds him by the sharpness of her speech and by her ungovernable temper; then she wonders why it is that she has no power in prayer.

There are other things in the relations of husbands and wives which doubtless are oftentimes a hindrance in approaching God in prayer. There is much of sin covered up under the holy name of marriage that is a cause of spiritual deadness and of powerlessness in prayer. Any man or woman whose prayers seem to bring no answer should spread their whole married life out before God, and ask Him to put His finger upon anything in it that is displeasing in His sight.

The seventh hindrance to prayer is found in James 1:5-7, "If any of you lacks wisdom, let him ask of God, who gives to all liberally and without reproach, and it will be given to him. But let him ask in faith, with no doubting, for he who doubts is like a wave of the sea driven and tossed by the wind. For let not that man suppose that he will receive anything from the Lord."

Prayers are hindered by unbelief. God demands that we shall believe His Word absolutely. To question it is to make Him a liar. Many of us do that when we plead His promises, and is it any wonder that our prayers are not answered? How many prayers are hindered by our wretched unbelief! We go to God and ask Him for something that is positively promised in His Word, and then we do not more than half expect to get it. "Let not that man suppose that he will receive anything from the Lord."

6.
INTERCESSION:
EVERY CHRISTIAN'S DUTY
GEORGE WHITEFIELD

Therefore I exhort first of all that supplications,
prayers, intercessions,
and giving of thanks be made for all men.
1 TIMOTHY 2:1

Why is there so little love to be found amongst Christians? Why is it the very characteristic by which everyone should know that we are disciples of the holy Jesus is almost banished out of the Christian world? We find the answer, in a great measure, owing to a neglect or superficial performance of that excellent part of prayer, *intercession*, or imploring the divine grace and mercy in behalf of others.

Some forget this duty of praying for others because they seldom remember to pray for themselves. Conversely, some of those who are constant in praying to their heavenly Father are so selfish in their addresses to the throne of grace that they do not enlarge their petitions for the welfare of their fellow Christians as they ought. They thereby fall short of attaining that Christian charity—that unfeigned love to their brethren which their sacred profession obliges them to aspire after—and without which, though they should bestow all their goods to feed the poor and even give their bodies to be burned, yet it would profit them nothing.

Since these things are so, I shall endeavor in this discussion to show two things: First, that it is every Christian's duty to pray for others as well as for himself.

Second, whom we ought to pray for and in what manner we should do it.

First, it is every Christian's duty to pray for others as well as for himself. Prayer is a duty founded on natural religion; the very heathens never neglected it, though many Christian heathens amongst us do. It is so essential to Christianity that you might as reasonably expect to find a living man without breath as a true Christian without the spirit of prayer and supplication.

Thus, no sooner was St. Paul converted,

but "behold, he is praying," said the Lord Almighty (Acts 9:11). And thus will it be with every child of God as soon as he becomes such: prayer being truly called the natural cry of the newborn soul.

In the heart of every true believer there is a heavenly tendency, a divine attraction, which as sensibly draws him to converse with God as the lodestone attracts the needle. A deep sense of their own weakness and of Christ's fullness; a strong conviction of their natural corruption and of the necessity of renewing grace will not let them rest from crying day and night to their Almighty Redeemer, that the divine image, which they lost in Adam, may through His all-powerful mediation and the sanctifying operation of His blessed Spirit be begun, carried on, and fully perfected both in their souls and bodies.

Thus earnest, thus persistent, are all sincere Christians in praying for themselves: But then, not having so lively, lasting, and deep a sense of the wants of their Christian brethren, they are for the most part too remiss and defective in their prayers for them. Whereas, was the love of God shed abroad in our hearts and did we love our neighbor in the manner in which the Son of God our Savior loved us, and according to His command and example, we could not but be as unrelenting in our prayers for their spiritual and temporal welfare as for our own; and as earnestly desire and endeavor that others should share in the benefits of the death and passion of Jesus Christ, as we ourselves.

Let not anyone think that this is an uncommon degree of charity, a high pitch of perfection, to which not everyone can attain; for, if we are all commanded to love our neighbor (that is every man) even as ourselves—nay, to lay down our lives for the brethren—then it is the duty of all to pray for our neighbors as much as for ourselves, and by all possible acts and expressions of love and affection toward them, at all times, to show our readiness even to lay down our lives for them, if ever it should please God to call us to it.

Our blessed Savior set an example for us in

that divine, that perfect and inimitable prayer recorded in the seventeenth chapter of John, which He put up just before His passion. In that prayer, we find but few petitions for His own sake, yet many for His disciples' welfare. Likewise, in that perfect form known as the Lord's Prayer, which He has been pleased to prescribe us, we are taught to say, not *my*, but *our Father*, thereby to put us in mind, that whenever we approach the throne of grace, we ought to pray not for ourselves alone, but for all our brethren in Christ.

Intercession then is certainly a duty incumbent upon all Christians.

Second, let us consider for whom we are to intercede and how this duty is to be performed. To begin, our intercession must be *universal*. St. Paul said, "I exhort first of all that supplications, prayers, intercessions. . .be made for all men" (1 Timothy 2:1). For as God's mercy is over all his works, as Jesus Christ died to redeem a people out of all nations and languages; so we should pray for "all men to be saved and to come to the knowledge of the truth" (2:4). Many precious promises are made in holy writ: that the gospel shall be published through the whole world, that "the earth shall be full of the knowledge of the LORD as the waters cover the sea" (Isaiah 11:9). Therefore, it is our duty not to confine our petitions to our own nation, but to pray that all those nations who now sit in darkness and in the shadow of death may have the glorious gospel shine out upon them, as well as upon us. But you need not that any man should teach you this, since you yourselves are taught of God, and of Jesus Christ Himself, to pray that His kingdom may come; part of the meaning of which petition is that God's "way may be known on earth, [and His] salvation among all nations" (Psalm 67:2).

Note that the *praying for all men extends to those who rule over us*; particularly for our national leaders, and all that are put in authority under them: that we may lead quiet lives, in all godliness and honesty.

For, if we consider how heavy the burden of government is and how much the welfare of any people depends on the zeal and godly conversation of those that have the rule over them; if we set before us the many dangers and difficulties to which governors by their station are exposed, and the continual temptations they be under to luxury and self-indulgence, we shall not only pity but pray for them. Let us pray that He who preserved Esther, David, and Josiah "unspotted from the world" (James 1:27), amidst the grandeur of a court, and gave success to their designs, would also preserve them holy and unblameable and prosper all the works of their hands upon them.

We need also to *pray for those whom "the Holy Spirit has made. . .overseers, to shepherd the church of God"* (Acts 20:28).

This is what St. Paul begs, again and again, of the churches to whom he writes: In both letters to the Thessalonians, he asks them, "Brethren, pray for us" (1 Thessalonians 5:25; 2 Thessalonians 3:1), and again, in Ephesians 6:18–19, "praying always with all prayer and supplication in the Spirit. . .and for me. . .that I may open my mouth boldly to make known the mystery of the gospel." And in another place, to express his earnestness in this request, and the great importance of their prayers for him, he bids the church to "strive [or, as the original word signifies, be in agony] together with me in prayers to God for me" (Romans 15:30). And surely, if the great St. Paul—that chosen vessel, that favorite of heaven—needed the most persistent prayers of his Christian converts, how much more do the ordinary ministers of the gospel stand in need of the intercession of their respective flocks.

I cannot but in a more especial manner insist upon this branch of your duty because it is a matter of such importance. I do not doubt that much good is frequently withheld from many, by reason of their neglecting to pray for their ministers; good which they would have received, had they prayed for them as they ought. Not to mention that people often complain of the want of diligent and faithful pastors.

But how do they deserve good pastors if they will not earnestly pray to God for such?

If we will not pray to the Lord of the harvest, can it be expected He will send forth laborers into His harvest?

Besides, what ingratitude is it, not to pray for your ministers! For shall they watch and labor in the Word and doctrine for you and your salvation, and shall not you pray for them in return? If any bestow favors on your bodies, you think it right, meet, and your bounden duty to pray for them; yet shall not they be remembered in your prayers, who daily feed and nourish your souls? Add to all this that praying for your ministers will be a manifest proof of your believing, that though Paul plant, and Apollos water, yet it is God alone who gives the increase. And you will also find it the best means you can use to promote your own welfare; because God, in answer to your prayers, may impart a double portion of His Holy Spirit to them, whereby they will be qualified to deal out to you larger measures of knowledge in spiritual things and be enabled more skillfully to divide the word of truth.

Would men but constantly observe this direction, and when their ministers are praying in their name to God, humbly beseech him to perform all their petitions; or, when they are speaking in God's name to them, pray that the Holy Ghost may fall on all them that hear the word, we should find a more visible good effect of their doctrine and a greater mutual love between ministers and their people. In so doing, those ministers' hands would then be held up by the people's intercessions, and the people will never dare to vilify or traduce those who are the constant subjects of their prayers.

Next to our ministers, *our friends claim a place in our intercessions*; but then we should not content ourselves with praying in general terms for them, but suit our prayers to their particular circumstances.

When Miriam was afflicted with leprosy from God, Moses cried and said, "Please heal her, O God, I pray!" (Numbers 12:13). And when the nobleman came to apply to Jesus Christ, in behalf of his child, he said, "My little daughter lies at the point of death. Come and lay Your hands on her, that she may be healed" (Mark 5:23). In like manner, when our friends are under any afflicting circumstances, we should endeavor to pray for them with a particular regard to those circumstances. For instance, is a friend sick? We should pray that if it be God's good pleasure, it may not be unto death; but if otherwise, that He would give him grace so to take his visitation, that, after this painful life ended, he may dwell with Him in life everlasting. Is a friend in doubt in an important matter? We should lay his case before God, as Moses did that of the daughters of Zelophehad (see Numbers 27), and pray that God's Holy Spirit may lead him into all truth and give all seasonable direction. Is he in want? We should pray that his faith may never fail and that in God's due time he may be relieved. And in all other cases, we should not pray for our friends only in general, but suit our petitions to their particular sufferings and afflictions; for otherwise, we may never ask perhaps for the things our friends most need.

It must be confessed that such a procedure

will oblige some often to break from the forms they use; but if we accustom ourselves to it and have a deep sense of what we ask for, the most illiterate will want proper words to express themselves.

We have many noble instances in holy scripture of the success of this kind of particular intercession, but none more remarkable than that of Abraham's servant in Genesis chapter 24, who, being sent to seek a wife for Abraham's son Isaac, prayed in a most particular manner. And the sequel of the story informs us how remarkably his prayer was answered. And did Christians now pray for their friends in the same particular manner and with the same faith as Abraham's servant did for his master, they would, no doubt, in many instances, receive as visible answers and have as much reason to bless God for them, as he had.

Furthermore, just as we ought thus to intercede for our friends, so in like manner must *we also pray for our enemies*. Jesus Himself tells us in Matthew 5:44, "Bless those who curse you. . .and pray for those who spitefully use you and persecute you." These commands He enforced in the strongest manner by His own example: In the very agonies and pangs of death, He prayed even for his murderers, "Father, forgive them, for they do not know what they do" (Luke 23:34). This, it must be confessed, is a difficult duty, yet not impracticable, to those who have renounced the things of this present life (from an inordinate love of which all enmities arise) and who, knowing the terrible woes denounced against those who offend Christ's little ones, can, out of real pity and a sense of their danger, pray for those by whom such offenses come.

Lastly, and to conclude this head, *we should intercede for all that are in any ways afflicted* in mind, body, or estate; for all who desire and stand in need of our prayers, and for all who do not pray for themselves.

And oh! That all who hear me would set apart some time every day for the due performance of this most necessary duty!